In a Layman's

Terms...

A practical guide to life in the

21st century

Scott E Rheuben

Contents

Your potential is exponential, but inconsequential, if you just sit

still!

"The truth is that our finest moments are most likely to occur

when we are feeling deeply uncomfortable, unhappy, or

unfulfilled. For it is only in such moments, propelled by our discomfort, that we are likely to step out of our ruts and start

searching for different ways or truer answers."

M. Scott Peck

(Going) Foreword

Firstly, I'd like to start by saying, I am not (or have never been), a CEO, Executive, business analyst, or an MBA graduate, and I have never run my own business. What I am, is someone who has worked overseas as well as in three states and one territory in Australia, working in almost 30 jobs, in a range of different fields, who has a great deal of lived experience. I studied Health Services Management (which led nowhere) followed by a Post-Graduate Certificate in Human Resource Management. I was disillusioned after university, and, having completed a course with no career pathway, I went back and did Human Resources (HR) because I had a passion for helping people. When I finished, back in 2002, there were no HR Generalist positions, it had all been outsourced into different areas, payroll, recruitment, and workplace health and safety. Anyway, I dabbled in each of these areas, dabbled, because I was never satisfied. It was no longer about people, it was just numbers, key performance indicators (KPI's), sales, prospective targets, efficiencies and cost-cutting, not incentives, career planning, recruitment, job retention and staff satisfaction. It was now a dog-eat-dog world, sell, sell, sell, justify your position, say this, do that. From the turn of the century, in line with the peak of capitalism, you were expected to compete against your colleagues, because when the numbers were crunched and someone had to go, they needed the person who could do the most, and who would complain the least.

The recruitment industry itself was no stranger to KPI's and predominantly operates by treating people as just another number. I've seen so many salespeople come into the recruitment game with no training or experience and so many talented compassionate trained people leaving their roles due to targets and commissions. Effectively, the industry is the same as real estate... or car sales. The more roles you fill, the bigger the commissions. Cold-calling, head-hunting, it's all on the table. Ethics and values play second fiddle. If the person you've placed leaves after a month, no-one cares. As I said before, I loved helping people find their right job, that was the right fit for everyone, but the game changed and I wasn't going to let my morals be brushed aside, so I did what I do when I'm not satisfied, I moved on to better things.

When I was young, I actually wanted to be a Careers Counsellor, well that and an Author, and this book, I guess, is a combination of both. It provides life advice and practical steps for managing your budget, changing your housing situation, applying for jobs, how to conduct yourself in an interview, how to break bad habits and how to change your path, to live the life you want to live. It also addresses life choices in final years of high school and pathways to get you on the right track. There is no wrong way, all choices provide lessons, but this book will hopefully help you reduce the number of U-turns and help you find YOUR best path.

According to the Australian Bureau of Statistics (ABS), the average weekly total earnings for individuals in Australians is $1,237.90

per week (or $64,407.94 per year)

https://www.abs.gov.au/ausstats/abs@.nsf/mf/6302.0 . Research

from McCrindle indicates that total **average household income is**

$109,668 in 2019 and since the mid 1990's "average household

gross incomes have increased 66% from $66,196 to $109,668,

while over the same period, incomes of the top 1 in 5 households

(highest quintile) have increased by 75% from $149,552 to

$261,872." **(https://mccrindle.com.au/insights/blog/australias-**

household-income-wealth-distribution). If you or your family are

at or above this mark, this book is probably not intended for you

(unless you need help finding a new job or managing your budget)

however a lot of people I know aren't anywhere near these

figures. When we hear these 'average' incomes they make us

cringe and we feel deflated and defeated. We think, if that's

average, what does that make me?

This book will not give you grand formulas and guarantees. I'm

going to try and give you a practical guide as to how to get things moving and how to work towards your goals. If you are not happy with where you are, let's get you to where you want to be! Some examples provided will be for those at a low point, simply trying to rent a house, find a job, manage a budget, get a loan, but these **principles**, when you follow them and form **routines,** are crucial, no matter what level you are at, or what level you are trying to achieve. Please be aware though, that these drastic changes won't happen overnight, quite often they will take time and perseverance. You need to show patience and discipline in following your new routine and not falling back into unhealthy habits. I've made many mistakes, so many I could not begin to count them all, however I have learnt a lot along the way, and I hope that this book will help you make some right decisions, avoid the pitfalls and help you get to where you want to be. **Don't be fearful of failure, that is the only way to learn.**

We must find what's missing, from deep inside, for what's a lion, without his pride?

Do You Know What You Want?

Do you... really? I know for a long time I thought I did. I was getting by, I made sure I was not without a job. I had a girlfriend (who became my wife) and we eventually got our first mortgage (I mean house), got married, and eventually had a family. I was happy (at home) but never satisfied with exactly 'what I wanted to do' for a living. Throughout this whole time, I had many different jobs, none of them provided any real job satisfaction, and it was only when I spent time writing, did I really feel satisfied. I knew that this is what I wanted to do for a living, but how was I ever really going to get there?

"If you don't know where you're going any road will get you there" Lewis Carroll

I was what some might say, lucky (or it was divinely coincidental), to have a lightbulb moment at the Byron Bay Writers Festival one year. Although I had written thousands of works of poetic verse, and had some published, in one solitary moment, I was provided with a new direction. At this festival someone asked the panel of Australia's best children's authors a question that changed my life. They asked if they just wrote whatever came out, or if they tried to have a moral message in their books. The panel unanimously, without a second thought all answered that they paid no heed to morals, they just wrote down what came out. I was shocked, I felt that there should at least be some attempt to provide a moral message to the youth of today. I felt (and still feel), that children are like sponges, and books seemed like such a good opportunity to help provide some direction. Surely there was some obligation to at least attempt to seize this moment? I didn't realise how strongly I had felt about it, until that question had been brought to light. From that moment, I decided that I was going to have a crack at writing children's books! Something that I had never thought about before, a new direction for me, happened within a few minutes. That started a motion, an idea, that led to creative manuscripts, and then the key words 'Roses are Not Red'. It came to me when I was asleep, I awoke with the words in my head and something telling me I needed to write it down. 99% of the time I would go back to sleep and forget it by the morning, but on this occasion, I wrote it down, and over the next few weeks, I had, what would become, my first published children's book. It flowed out of me in a torrent, I was just the conduit, and the words couldn't get onto the page quickly enough. I was open, spiritually awake, and I was ready, and I just wrote it all down.

"A man without a purpose is like a ship without a rudder"

Thomas Carlyle

Once you've got some direction it is important to plan ahead, but being motivated to take each small step is even more important. You must learn to accept rejection. Being a writer is a perfect example. I have put forward close to a hundred submissions of work to publishing companies, 99% of them don't even send a reply. Not even a generic response, nada. It does dent your confidence I will not deny it, but it is that 'I'm not going to be defeated' attitude that will help you succeed, if not in that venture, then the next best thing that comes along, that might be even better than the first. Don't fear rejection, it is just a part of the process.

"Not until we are lost, do we begin to understand ourselves"

Henry Thoreau

Take the First Step – NOW!

"It's much more important to start, than to be smart" Scott Pape

The first step is the hardest (and most important), and then the next, followed by the one after that, but **if you don't start the change process, the process won't change**. Bad habits form routines, and if left unchecked, lead you into comfortable patterns. This same cycle you may have been in for months, years, even decades! Most research suggests that it usually takes between 1 and 2 months to break a habit, however, depending on the individual, the process can be *'as few as 18 days or up to 250 days'* (https://www.wikihow.com/Break-a-Habit). We all have bad habits we need to curb. I still chew my nails, some people grind their teeth, whatever it is, we need to get back in control and stop these behaviours. If you have bad habits like biting your lip, you can try applying a bad-tasting lip balm to keep you from biting. You need to substitute bad behaviour with other things you like doing. Put on your favourite music, play with your children, or take the dog for a walk, just don't substitute one bad habit for another, (i.e. don't substitute gambling, with over-eating). Reward yourself when you accomplish resisting this bad habit. Nobody's perfect and we all let ourselves slip sometimes, but we need discipline, particularly when you want to move forward and reposition your life. Break the bad habits and you will break the cycle and trajectory that your life is on.

"God grant me the serenity to accept the things I cannot change, the courage to change the things I can and the wisdom to know the difference" Reinhold Niebuhr

If you are not in the place you want to be, you need to first break bad habits by changing the regular patterns in your life. It will be hard, like a recovering addict from smoking or alcohol, the withdrawals of your previous everyday routines, as well as your self-doubt saying, "why are you even bothering, you won't be able to do this," will be hard to conquer. You will only be able to do this by **taking one step at a time, one moment at a time,** and then the next, and then the next. It may take some time, weeks, sometimes even months, but you need to **stick with it, till it becomes your 'new routine'**. Once you start, you need to stay the course. Show discipline until new doors open.

"The only place success comes before work, is in the dictionary"
Vince Lombardi

"Circumstances do not make the man, they reveal him" James Allen

Time is Not Money, Time is Opportunity

"Don't wait. The time will never be just right" Napoleon Hill

Sometimes, you've just to **put yourself in that position**, to give yourself the opportunity. Whether you believe in coincidence, luck, or just good timing, you've got to be in it to win it. Sometimes the hardest thing is taking that first step. You will have self-doubts, 'I'm not good enough', 'someone else with more experience will apply', 'I don't have this',' I don't have that'... Just do it! You might miss out on that particular role however, they may have another role that they are also about to recruit for, and that you would be perfect for. They might get no other applications, the system may have been down, or applications somehow deleted, who knows the situation, but if you never put your application in, you will never be in with a chance. A slim chance is better than none, and even if you miss out on the role, the feedback you might get, might be just what you need to secure your next job, or your next contract.

Put yourself in a position that is ready for each prospect that comes your way. You need to be ready to go when each new opportunity presents itself. If it's a job, have you done your research about the company? What direction are they headed, is it a growth industry? Will you get bored, will it challenge you? Do you want to be challenged? Is it a position that is likely to be replaced by automation in 3 years, 5 years? If so, how can you up-skill to be one of the people that becomes necessary when many of the positions are replaced? Perhaps you can undertake some training, but you also need to always be willing to put up your hand for extra duties. **Once you get yourself in a position where you are invaluable, you will make yourself irreplaceable**. Even if the time comes where you are not offered further employment, hopefully you have proven yourself enough, to get an excellent reference, and be able to find something else easily enough.

'To everything there is a season, and a time to every purpose under the heaven: A time to be born, and a time to die; a time to

plant, and a time to pluck up that which is planted ... A time to

weep, and a time to laugh; a time to mourn, and a time to dance

... A time to rend, and a time to sew; a time to keep silence, and

a time to speak' Book of Ecclesiastes Chapter 3

Be prepared. Give yourself some quiet time to plan what steps

you need to take. Will the new bank you are applying for a loan

with, need to assess credit rating, previous statements, credit

card debts, other debts, letter of support from real estate? Expect

banks to want to know everything about you, breaks in

employment, a bad rental history, everything! They want to

minimise risk, especially these days, so you might need a

guarantor (possibly parents), or some evidence that you can pay

back debts (i.e. at least 6 months of repayment history) before

applying for any type of loan.

Timing is essential. If you want to go and study whether it be Tafe

or University, they will have specific key dates in which they accept enrolments (similar to School). Don't think you can just start at any time (though some online courses do allow this). Do your research, plan early in the year as some units may only have an intake once a year, and if you miss enrolment by a day it could mean, you'll be waiting till next year!

Stay Focused

Keep your eye on the prize. If you want something whether it be new job, new house, new car, or just new clothes, you need to **stay focused**. Do the hard yards, pre-plan, and do a brainstorming exercise where you jot down all activities that you can do to help you get there. **Write down what it is that you want.** Sometimes finding a picture of exactly what you want, can help. If so, put it up somewhere in your room. It will provide a reminder as to why you are getting up at 5am, or still working on job applications at 11pm at night. **Work to your strengths**. If you are a morning person, start early. If you are a night owl, put in a lot of hours at night. If you can put this into **a daily or weekly schedule**, this will also help you stick to the plan. Remember, focus on what you want, and show persistence in working towards it. Sometimes you have to find another way to get a start, so you will **also need to be flexible**. Speak to those who are in the place you want to be, learn from them, but find your own way. We can never just follow one path; we need to **learn the skills** so that we can have the ability to find our own way of reaching our potential. It is good to have a dream (or goal), but without action – it will always be out of reach. You need to **show courage** to take your first steps on this journey, and **persist**, no matter how much people doubt you. You must face your own self-doubts, and be willing to do it the hard way.

"Do not fear mistakes – there are none" Miles Davis

Are You Paying Attention?

Be Present – stay focused when speaking to someone. Is your mind wandering? Are you thinking of what your friend is up to, what you can have for dinner, or what's happening tomorrow? Try and focus on what is directly in front of you. Don't worry about the future or keep thinking about what has happened in the past. Your life and your ability to shape your future, happens every second, every heartbeat. Raise your awareness, stay calm and focused and good things will come your way.

"The quality of life is in proportion, always to capacity for delight. The capacity for delight is the gift of paying attention"
Julia Cameron

Pay attention to gut instincts. Don't trust everything you hear. If you get given advice, but the advice is not going to work for you, or doesn't FEEL right, take it with a grain of salt. If something doesn't feel right, whether it be a rental property, a job, a car, business opportunity… don't do it! You've got to trust your gut instincts as often as you can. Don't be fearful. You need to recognise what is just you worrying about doing something different, and what seems like a bad option for you. Sometimes you won't know the difference, as you have such an ingrained fear of giving something a go. In these situations, get a second opinion. Perhaps this will confirm your doubts, or dissolve them, so that you can steer yourself in a new direction. I'm not talking about getting nervous, worried about debt, concerned about a bossy manager, I'm talking about a primal instinctive knowing, that something is just not for you. You will know deep down when something is not sitting well with you – always trust your gut. No-one knows what is best for you, better than you!

"Every time you don't follow your inner guidance, you feel a loss of energy, loss of power, a sense of spiritual deadness" Shakti Gawain

Find your balance. Life is hard at times, no harder or easier than our forefathers (it is all relative), we just have different challenges. Sometimes we need a break. This might be going part-time, having an extended break, maybe you have been working overtime to achieve a deadline. Perhaps your partner is now going back to work, so you might be able to see if you can drop a shift. Have a plan in place, it might be working two jobs for a short period, or going part-time and doing some part-time study to help you towards your dream job. Maybe it's moving interstate to stay with your cousin and look for opportunities there. Whatever is best to improve your quality of life (and your family's) you need to follow this path.

There is no square. Stop thinking that you just need to tick the box, or follow the standard way and things will fall into place. You need to think outside of any boundaries or restrictions. Be flexible; how creative can you be? In regards to finding a job perhaps you could volunteer, or offer your potential employer an unpaid work trial, just to get a start. Does the employer have a casual register? Most of my colleagues, and I, gained employment at the University by initially getting a start as a casual. This is also often the case for disability support roles, as well as many opportunities in government roles.

"For true success ask yourself these four questions, Why? Why Not? Why Not Me? Why Not Now?" James Allen

What is The State of Play?

If it's a house to buy, or rent, have you looked at current market prices? Is there a downturn? How long has the property been listed? Speak to real estate agents and local publicans, and listen to their opinions! Is there public transport, or a new school or shopping centre being built around the corner? How will that affect prices if you are renting? Perhaps this will push prices up, which will not be good for you. Are there a lot of houses selling in the same area? If so, why? If you're really interested in buying a particular property, have you been to the bank, and know exactly what they will lend you? Before making an offer, have you done pest and building inspection? The last step will be to arrange a lawyer, to look over the contract, and then ... the final negotiations. Know the market prices and make an offer that is appropriate for that property. If you live in a city you might have to offer the going rate (or sometimes higher) just to get a look in. You will need to be quick and have your finances in order. **If you don't live in the city don't ever offer the price that is listed.** Australia lacks the negotiation and bartering of other countries but real estate is one of the few chances (as a buyer) to haggle on price. It's all about supply and demand, and with many buyers looking, particularly at the low-end of the market, you need to be ready. One rule applies though whenever you are buying a property, whether you are buying at an auction, or making an offer after an open house, **be prepared, know what you can afford, and don't go beyond your financial limits**.

Do Your Research

Learn more about what you are focused on and interested in. Read books, and always ask questions. You need to **build your knowledge** on the areas that you want to change. Start by asking people you trust, whether it's friends, or family, find out what they know, and heed any advice that may be relevant. Like all advice, sift through it and only take what you need. If the person is putting you down, or not providing information of any assistance, ask someone else. Write a list of people who might be able to assist. For example, you can do a google search and find out who offers courses in automotive repairs in your local area, or look up local real estate agents and write them all down so that you can go in and start getting rental lists. You can look online for real estate at larger sites like realestate.com. au, or check on the gumtree website, or other local sites. When looking at buying a house, do research for real estate look up sites like onthehouse.com.au (which gives you a rough estimate on price). For getting a new car, check out sites like redbook.com, or comparethemarket sites for comparing interest rates etc.

If you want to pursue a career in a particular area, what are the prerequisites for the jobs that you are interested in? Is there a course you need to do? Ask someone who is already in the role. Be brave, what have you got to lose? Most people will do all they can to point you in the right direction. Do you want to change your current predicament? Do you really? In the movie "The Pursuit of Happyness" Will Smith perfectly illustrates what it takes, to provide a new life for his son, saying, "you want something go get it... period." How far or how hard are you willing to go, to change YOUR life?

When looking at buying a product, compare what is available and then you can go in to the relevant store and see if they can do a better deal. **In each situation, be sure to get a second opinion.** For example, if you are looking at used cars, you can do research online, write down the best options on paper and then you can go to the caryard and see if they have anything similar that can beat those prices. If you need a tradesman to do some work on your place, get quotes from at least two of them, so that you know you are not getting ripped off. If you are going on a holiday, look online at best prices, then you can call the local travel agent let them know what dates etc you are looking at and what price you have found yourself, and see if they can beat it! Sometimes they have wholesale prices that general consumers are not privy to. This is the same thing with getting a loan, compare interest rates online (as well as all general fees) and then shop around, either make the calls, or do the walk around town and drop in (depending on what will be quickest). **Remember it all starts with doing your research, seeing what is on offer, and then, seeing who is negotiable, to get you the best deal.** This is not an easy thing to do, but it is an important skill to have, especially if you lack confidence and need help improving your communication skills. What is the worst that can happen, the person will end up saying, 'sorry I can't beat that price'? Negotiation skills are important in many jobs, and it is especially useful if you have the opportunity to go overseas. In many countries, a lot of general day-to-day items in markets (and even in shopping centres) are negotiable on price. Another thing to note, you are only buying a car, or changing banks, or negotiating your insurance realistically every couple of years (at most), so give it a go and when you secure a good deal, it will help you improve your confidence and raise your self-esteem.

"Do or do not, there is no try" Yoda

Know Your Product

If you want to buy a car, give strong consideration to buying one second-hand, rather than getting a loan for a new one. It is often said that most cars will lose at least 20% of their value the second that you drive it out of the dealership. When buying a car, motorbike etc, if you don't know what questions to ask, particularly if you are buying second hand, you need to know what you are looking for in regards to engines, makes, and bad models. Perhaps there is someone who can go with you who knows more about these things? Is there a service book showing regular services? When was it last serviced? Is this particular model one that has a history of being faulty or unreliable? Why is the person selling**? What seems like a deal that is too good to be true, usually is**. Don't be afraid to say you'll have a think about it.

Don't impulse buy. Whether it's expensive items or just grocery shopping when you are hungry, you will end up with things you don't particularly need.

Current Trends, Current Progress

Notice different opportunities that are happening in your local community i.e. is there a new shopping centre being built, maybe a highway upgrade? Find out which retail outlets are moving in. Perhaps you might want to get your traffic control ticket, and find out which construction company has the contract, if that's what you are interested in. By keeping up with what's happening in, and around your local area, you will be able to be prepared for opportunities as they become available. Further to this, if you are in the construction game you will need to know which companies have the contract for new projects and where they will be taking place. Always keep up to date on emerging industries, growth areas, or, who has the next big project that you would like to be working on.

If you haven't already noticed, we are in the midst of a Housing crisis in Australia with not enough affordable housing. In response to the social housing crisis in Australia new programs are constantly emerging. For example, 'Opportunity Pathways' is a new program that is designed to break the cycle of disadvantage for social housing recipients which will also reduce their reliance on government-funded social housing or Rent Choice subsidies. This program will help clients have greater housing independence while also providing practical and financial assistance, training and work opportunities to help them prepare for employment, find a job or improve their employment options. This is just one of many new programs that will support those in social housing to break their cycle, and get ahead in life, and at the same time, it illustrates newly emerging employment opportunities. These new roles such as Employment and Housing Support Worker, and

Community Engagement Coordinators, were not around, even a few years ago. The community services sector is one area that will continue to change and evolve over the next decade. Some industries will grow, some will decline, **but you need to have some awareness that industries that require individualised personal service, and roles that require critical thinking and analysis, flexibility and creativity, will continue to be required, no matter how rapid the rise of automation is.** Always keep your eyes out for new emerging industries, and others that are being reduced. Such industries as print media have had to adapt and change to ensure that they have an online presence and all industries are facing challenges each and every day.

Be Persistent

"The one who falls and gets up is so much stronger than the one who never fell" **Roy** T Bennett

I applied for 30 jobs at the university before getting a permanent job there. Ironically, while I was working in HR, I overheard other staff laughing about a perennial applier who had put in around a dozen applications. What did that make me? I could have sat back and felt dejected, or given up after the first or second attempt, too ashamed to apply for other roles, but I didn't. I am too determined, and persistent (my wife might say stubborn), but this is the only way to be, to get what you want. You must always be willing to give things a go. Don't think twice. Persistence is hard because there is a fine line between persisting with something that may get you somewhere, (i.e. gym work to be a bodybuilder) and persisting with something that will only lead to more knockbacks (i.e. continuing to send through the same manuscript to the same publisher and expecting a positive response). *"The definition of insanity is doing the same thing over and over and expecting different results."* (unknown author). In regards to sending through the manuscript it could be worth persisting with the fundamentals of the story while making a few significant changes in the manuscript (including a cover letter) and sending it through again. Alternatively, subtle changes like a different style, or changing a central character, may make all the difference. You cannot let one defeat, or one rejection lead you away from what you are passionate about.

"Courage doesn't always roar. Sometimes courage is that quiet voice at the end of the day saying, 'I will try again tomorrow"
Mary Anne Radmacher

There will be many challenges in trying to do what you love, but persistence is key, if you really want it badly enough. You've got to keep picking yourself up and dusting yourself off, that is the only way you'll get to where your heart desires.

"Success is going from failure to failure with no loss of enthusiasm" Winston Churchill

"Patience, persistence and perspiration make an unbeatable combination for success" Napoleon Hill

Keep moving – you need to try, try, and try again. Take any positive feedback or lessons that you can learn from each unsuccessful attempt. You can take the time to be upset, disappointed or even angry, but the sooner you pick yourself up, and try again, the sooner you will take the next important step in your life.

"I can accept failure. Everyone fails at something. But I can't accept not trying" Michael Jordan

You've got to have that hunger, to do what it takes to get yourself to where you want to be. I'm not talking about watching a motivational video on YouTube and feeling energised for the next hour. It must be something deep and resonating within your heart and soul. The whole reason you are here. Your purpose; to be happy and to live to your potential.

Be Flexible

I spent almost 25 years writing poetic verse. One genre, thousands of songs/verses. Sure, it offered me an outlet for expression of my feelings, and sure, I did get 2 books published (my first book publisher went into liquidation, and both books have cost me money and not made me any) but I barely branched out. Finally, I turned my hand at another genre, and spent a year on a fantasy/adventure novel based off star sign characters. 'The Battle of Chi' was the end result, which became an e-book. Once again, I tried to get it published, but no luck. I still think it is a great book, but the time it took to create, and the joy it brought compared to when I later wrote children's books, was no comparison. Still, it was my first change from poetic verse, and perhaps if I'd had a go at different genres earlier, I would have found my calling a lot sooner. I have now written more than twenty children's books (although only 1 is published). While I don't call myself an author, (that insinuates making money from books) I do call myself a writer. My paid job is in disability services, however, I will still keep submitting books to publishers, until hopefully I achieve my dream of writing for a living. The message from this is, make sure that you acquire new skills and build your knowledge. Put your hand up for upskilling, or short-term roles within your organisation. If you are a cleaner and they need someone for stocktake, raise your hand. It might seem like it is not going to lead to anything, but the company might be going to sub-contract their cleaning to another company, and only continue with a stocktake person. With some experience under your belt, it is likely that they will just keep you on as that person. Never doubt the unseen hand of fate, and how taking opportunities, leads to good fortune. If there are opportunities in your organisation to work away, at another location, this may allow you to build networks or contacts that will lead you to other openings. If you are in the creative industries, try as many forms (or genres) until you find your niche, and until something clicks, however, always be willing to try something new and challenge yourself. Be flexible, and keep going. There will be many knockbacks, no matter what it is you are looking for. Having hobbies and trying different techniques or roles, even in the same industry, leads to a larger skill base which also makes you more employable.

"What if I fall? Oh, but my darling, what if you fly?" Erin Hanson

How Are You Going to Get There?

"Make your own recovery the first priority in your life" Robin Norwood

When we're in a rut, or can't seem to make any progress we need to follow a **process for change.**

HOMEWORK:

- **Write down where you want to be and what you want to do** in 1 year, 3 years and 5 years time. Maybe you want to study this year, be working and studying within 3 years, and finding your own place within 5 years. Whatever it is, put it down on paper. Be as specific as you can – these are the goals you will be working towards.

- **Be accountable for your actions. Take responsibility**. Perhaps your parents were poor, maybe you have never had any new clothes to wear. Let it go. Don't be bound to your past, with your current lot in life. Take a deep breath and repeat after me. *"From now on I am my own person. I will walk my own path and not feel entitled, or feel that anyone owes me anything. I will achieve what I want to,* *based on effort and persistence."* This independence is crucial to growth.

- **Learn from past mistakes**. We all make mistakes, all the time. The secret is to learn from them, so that you improve and begin to move beyond obstacles and increase your knowledge. These are your stepping stones to success.

- **Keep moving forward.** One step at a time. It is the only way to get where you want to. Creighton Williams Abrams Jr once said *"how do you eat an elephant ....one bite at a time"* (please don't go and start eating elephants). Paul Kelly's words *"from little things, big things grow"* might be more appropriate. In Sanskrit reference is made to *'padam, padam'* (which translates to, *step by step*). Take subtle steps to improve yourself, and keep moving forward. **After intention you need movement, with movement we create change. Show**

disciple towards the above steps, and you can be anything you want to be.

If you need help with your discipline, do a **weekly plan** and work out activities that you are going to do each day. For example, you might do job search, in morning, house searching in the afternoon. Perhaps during lunch, you might phone a friend who has recently been through a similar situation. Ask questions, do research online, get everything sorted out, resume, references (for real estate or work), **preparation is key!**

If the above does not work for you, another way to identify your blueprint for success is to identify smart goals. These are often used in business all across the globe, to map out a pathway to success, and they can be used by you as well.

SMART Goals

Specific – i.e. it might be something like, "get my licence before the end of the year"

Measurable – you must be able to determine if the goal has been achieved (e.g. getting licence in example above).

Achievable - Don't be unrealistic and say in your yearly goal that you want to be an astronaut. You might enrol in, and start a course, that will help get you there though.

Relevant -how is each step relevant and realistic to get where you want to?

Time-based - what timeframe is the goal/s to be achieved by?

After you've done this (and building on this process), get a spreadsheet, or divide a piece of paper into 5 columns, titled **MY SUCCESS PLAN** which has a range of tasks you need to do. In the first column write: *Goals*, second column, *Actions Required*. Third column – *Support From* (if applicable), fourth column – *Follow up* (once again if applicable) and maybe a fifth column *Feedback*. This can be another source or contact given that you can use if you have no success with these tasks.

An example might be – **Goal** – find accommodation

 Action required – check newspapers, get listings from local real estates, ask friends, put application at Community Housing (if this is a consideration for you).

Support from – e.g. best friend, uncle, support worker

Follow up – support worker will be back on 1/4/2020 or, left message for your mate Bob to get the number for your previous real estate who might be able to do a reference for your previous rental.

Feedback – The house you like is available in 2 months, get another reference. Bob might also have spare room in a few weeks (will need to call him on Monday to find out). Write It down. This way you won't forget where everything's up to. Obviously if you have a photographic memory you won't need to write things down, but for the rest of us, get a writing book, to

keep track of your progress.

GOAL	ACTION REQUIRED	SUPPORT FROM	FOLLOW UP	FEEDBACK
Find house	Check newspapers			
	Listings from real estates			
	Ask friends	Mate Bob Uncle Support worker	Left Msg 20/3/20 Called 19/3/20. To call back 1/4/20	Call again.
	Put application in at community			

	housing			

If you need to, you can put down another column (after *Action Required*) which is *Action By*. This might be useful for those who struggle with not only getting started, but those who need motivation in regards to completing certain activities. This might be, by tomorrow, next week, end of the month, but if you are working with the timeframes, make sure you stick to it, or if you miss a deadline, that activity becomes priority BY TODAY, or BY TOMORROW!

Reward yourself – if you've just been to the bank to ask about a personal loan, or done the shopping, or got a rental list and arranged some appointments, congratulate yourself, you have taken some steps to improve or change your current situation. I'm not saying go and get drunk, just take a breath and acknowledge that you are on the right track. By doing these steps for each major goal that you have, you will be able to clearly see what actions you have taken, which will keep you in a positive mindset. This will help you remain calm and focused and it won't be long before you achieve a breakthrough.

Listen to Others Advice

Don't be embarrassed to ask for advice. Learn as much as you can on your own, but when you are stuck make sure you don't just let it all slide, keep the momentum going. Listen to friends who have been in similar situations, ask family, just **don't be too proud to ask for help.** People want to help other people, it is natural, and if they can't help, they will hopefully point you in the right direction. Once again, for those who only offer negative comments and not constructive feedback, simply ignore what they say. Usually this will be people who are too afraid to try to break their own cycle and don't want you to make a step forward. This will be covered further in the chapter – *Support Cast.*

Arrange an appointment with a financial adviser. Quite often first visits are free, and this can sometimes be the case for legal advice also. Make sure though that you have all your questions ready and that you have done all the preparation that you can possibly do, so that you can maximise this 'free' advice.

(During) and After School

This was always going to be a key part of this book; what next after school? How do you even begin to imagine what's out there, outside of this bubble, called School? *'My parents don't have a clue; they didn't even have computers back then?'* most of you will say. A lot has changed, and a lot will continue to change, but you need to know your options. I know most people I've spoken to were barely given any advice from their school counsellor, just 'study Maths and some English and study hard! Everything depends on your final grades'. While in your final High School years the best advice is to **try many different things, and challenge yourself**. Also, I will let you in on one of the biggest secrets that I wish I knew going through high school.... are you ready? **Your results in high school won't define you, and it is no big deal if you miss out on getting the score you need**. I'm not saying they're not important, but you don't need to lose sleep or feel as pressured, as you have been told you need to be. No matter what the teachers tell you and how daunting the high school certificate is, there are always other options to get into further studies or apprenticeships, or whatever you want to do. **Pick subjects that you really enjoy**; you don't even need to know what career opportunities there are in that area. It will open doors for you and small opportunities will come to light in due course. You need to follow your heart, don't get redirected into subjects that don't interest you, that may have more 'prospects' career-wise. This re-direction might be from teachers, careers counsellors, family or friends who are trying to look out for your best interests. Heed their advice, particularly if you are not sure what you want to do, but if there are subjects at school that you really enjoy, whether it be a language, ancient history, or music, make sure you stick with them.

There are many paths to get you where you want to go

Unfortunately, the one major thing they neglect to tell you in high school is that if you don't have excellent grades, you can still go on to university (and even be a doctor or scientist). It will just be a different path to get there. Most universities have pathway programs, that you can undertake, and, depending on your grade, can lead you into almost any degree. Alternatively, you can do another course and then achieve a certain grade point average (GPA) and transfer to the course you want, after six or twelve months. If only they'd told you that at school, you wouldn't have had to feel the most intense pressure, as if your life was over, if you didn't get the mark you wanted! Don't get overly stressed, there are many roads to where you might want to go. It's not worth getting worked up over. Just choose what interests you and do your best and a path will become clear at some stage.

If your interest lies in blue-collar work, getting a trade as an electrician, builder, plumber, mechanic, chef, or maybe a massage therapist, you can leave school after year 10 and get an apprenticeship or traineeship as soon as you can. Or, ideally, you can do a school-based apprenticeship. This period of time is perhaps more important for the person considering a trade, rather than the student staying on through years 11 and 12. **If you are doing an apprenticeship, make sure you complete it!** If you get halfway through and give up, and then can't find another opportunity, it will make things a bit of a struggle for you, down the track. You might not get recognition for what you have completed, and you will likely have to start from the beginning when you do re-commit.

Another of these options, while in school, is a program called Head-Start (although it may have had a name-change). This pathway provides an opportunity for Year 11 and 12 students to gain direct entry and advanced standing into a variety of courses offered at University courses while still completing high school. One of the positives is that the program is free from university fees, while offering a chance to get a taste of university life, and see if university is something that you want to consider doing. Alternatively, as mentioned above, there are also traineeships and apprenticeships you can do while at high school, if you know what area you would like to be in, or internships that might be offered after students have undertaken some work experience (either during or after your school years), so the choice for your work experience can be crucial.

Make sure you don't waste your work experience. This is the perfect chance to contact a local employer in a subject area that you have a keen interest, whether it be photography, radio, theatre production, engineering, veterinary, or nursery work, this is an opportunity not to be wasted. Be brave and ambitious with whatever this choice might be, as it may help redirect or reinforce the direction that you want to go in, and if you love it and do well, you may get offered an internship or ongoing employment.

"The beautiful thing about learning is nobody can take it away from you" B.B King

You don't need to go to university or excel in your endeavours from an early age. Michael Jordan couldn't make his high school basketball team in his second year of high school. High school drop-outs such as Walt Disney, Humphrey Bogart, Richard Branson and, university drop-out, Steve Jobs, also left their personal mark on the world without taking a traditional path. Don't be disheartened if you don't follow a traditional pathway to your personal success.

Are you considering a gap or break year? If you're a young person who has never travelled; **travel.** Work abroad or interstate, or simply just take a break straight after school. You need to see what the world has to offer. If you want to jump straight into work after school - **work elsewhere, away from home! Go as far and wide as your circumstances allow.** Move to another town, another state, another country if you can! You may come back, but you'll have more to offer when you do. I will talk further about anchors in other chapters however, it is a lot easier to travel without commitments, either your child's schooling, sports or arts activities, or just watering a garden, or owning a pet. Travel young, if you can. If you can't travel young, **do it as soon as you can!** There's a whole world of opportunity out there waiting for you! **Allow for a change of environment – see what opportunities come your way and you'll find the next step.**

Trying to predict where the jobs will be

Without being given some advice, or getting out there, you will never know. If you're in school, do the subjects you want to do. Don't make adjustments because you are trying to predict future available jobs. Stick with units you love doing, and, if you stay on the path, you will find a job you never knew existed and that you never would have dreamed of. If there is something you love doing, make sure you stick with it! You want to keep your heart satisfied and nourished as much as you can. You don't want to have regrets in 20 years about not giving something a go because you wanted 'security' or a 'traditional path'. Your passion and your conscience should be your compass, and your most valued guide.

What is Your Passion?

What is your passion? What do you love doing? What inspires you? If you don't know, you are lost, and you need to find out. If you are not passionate about anything, you will need to look harder to find what you love doing, and what might lead you on a path that will provide you with a satisfied life. For example, if you like comics, have you ever tried to draw? Maybe you've liked books about trucks, perhaps being a truck driver, or a mechanic might be your thing? If you're a gamer, maybe you can create software, or be a salesman, because you know the product so well. Explore every prospect that makes your heart flutter. You might just love listening to music. Get an instrument, learn to play, see what happens when you give it a go. If you don't try to find what it is your soul desires, you will constantly be unsatisfied.

"The poor man is not he who is without a cent, but he who is without a dream" Harry Kemp

How Much Time are You Wasting?

Escape technology's trap. Get off Facebook, YouTube, Instagram, Snapchat, Tinder, Twitter, whatever you are using. You need to try and go without it, or, at least find a way to limit it. If it is TV or Netflix that takes your fancy, you must keep this in check. **You will never achieve your soul purpose in front of a screen.** Get back to nature, walk, ride, swim, dance, play a musical instrument, read a book, do something! Get out and talk to real people; join a club, volunteer, play a sport, do craft, or maybe philosophy? Any of these activities that you enjoy will lead to a greater connection with yourself and your community. This will allow the new, more focused, and positive you, to reveal yourself while rapidly enhancing your self-development. These new activities will provide a lesson in reality, which will also help you identify what people's real struggles and triumphs are, and how they manage to deal with them. Conversations and communication with people you wouldn't expect to be in contact with, will widen your perspective and perhaps lead to new friendships. The alternative is the same old boring you, who doesn't even have the time or energy to leave the house. **Don't just keep playing the victim, it's not making you happy**.

"If you can't fly then run, if you can't run then walk, if you can't walk then crawl, but whatever you do, you have to keep moving forward" Martin Luther King Jr.

If you have a child, spend time just sitting with them, listening to them, and teaching them. Get off your phone, don't answer that call (unless it's about a job), spend an hour a day talking to your partner, spending time with your family, away from the radio, TV and Internet, and see the positive changes that take place. So much of our real human connection in face-to-face contact has been lost with the growing pandemic of technology. Skype is great for friends and family overseas, however, if there is someone you can go and visit, make the effort to go and see them in the flesh. Make time for your family and friends. Meet and talk as much as possible before you lose your ability to interact at a comfortable level in social environments. This phenomenon is already happening and has been virtually in parallel lines with the rise of gaming and time spent online. Some kids and young adults come out of their home environment and don't know how to interact on any social level. Break the cycle, breath the fresh air, and notice the beauty of nature. What have you got to show for the hours of gaming, or Netflix that you have been spending your time on? Sure, we all need downtime; some TV, Facebook, YouTube, Instagram, Xbox, Netflix, whatever it is, but we need to keep it in check. If you are on Facebook, two hours a day, that is at least one and a half hours too long.

"Be always resolute with the present hour. Every moment is of infinite value; for it is the representative of eternity" Johann Wolfgang Von Goethe

HOMEWORK:

Find some time to **do something without technology...**

disconnect!

Repeat it until it becomes a routine and you will break your TV or internet habit.

Take responsibility for your actions. Don't look for someone else to blame.

You also need to know that all of **your actions have consequences**. It doesn't matter if it's eating that doughnut, placing a bet on the races, drinking that beer, lazing about. Every action has an equal and opposite reaction. While you have two feet and a heartbeat, you need to make something of your time in this world. Stop procrastinating – start taking action! *While there is life there is breath, and I will use mine, until death.*

Support Cast

"It's better to walk alone, than with a crowd going in the wrong direction" Diane Grant

Don't listen to those saying, "why bother", "have another drink" or "it'll get you nowhere." Where do you think you are? Is it really where you want to be? These so-called 'friends' are comfortable in their cycle of self-pity, and are happy going nowhere. If you sit back down and agree with their opinions, you can throw this book out now. **The only person who can change you, is you**. You decide where you want to get to, what you want to do, where you want to go. Don't blame anyone else for your current predicament. It's not your mum, your dad, your siblings, or even your friends' fault; you have walked this path. If you have had a tough life, use it as a strength, **your greatest weakness, is also your greatest strength**. No one else may have sat at rock bottom. Knowing what it is like, you will want to work harder for opportunities because you don't want to go back to where you were!

"The greater your storm, the brighter your rainbow" Anonymous

Don't go Backwards, Only Forwards.

Some old friends will get jealous of you when you get regular work, and have more money coming in. They might expect you to shout drinks, or contribute more etc. Don't let this happen. Move away from those who won't support you, anyone who is constantly putting you down, or people who are providing a negative influence in your life. Some of these so-called friends will try to blackmail you by saying that you don't spend time with them, and that you are not helping them out. If any of this is occurring, it's time to find new friends. If you live with them, it's time to find a new place to live. It's like an abusive relationship, you've got to cut it loose. There is no benefit to you, or them. By you moving onwards and upwards, you are shining a path and blazing a way for them. When they are ready, they will come and ask you for advice. If it doesn't happen, **that is their decision!** Take the lead, when those closest to you aren't willing to. If they give you a hard time, as scary as it seems, get out there and find new people who will love and respect, the new you. If you are moving in a different direction you need to find your own way and build new networks of people who will provide a positive influence. These people will help you on your way to building a new life for yourself and provide encouragement and direction along the way. They will be your new support network.

"Never look back unless you are planning to go that way"

Henry Thoreau

Have the Courage to Step Out on Your Own

You need to learn to be on your own, to put self-doubt behind

you. To step bravely out of the shadows, and cast your own.

There is no set path for you to walk, no silver bullet, no blueprint.

You will face obstacles that no-one else will, (don't worry, they

will have their own), but you cannot wallow in self-pity - you need

to keep moving forward. It's always darkest before the dawn,

however as *Edward Fitzgerald* once said **"this too shall pass"**.

"Life shrinks or expands in proportion to one's courage" Anais

Nin

Caught between a rock and a hard place ... you'd better mind

the jagged edges!

Break out of your shelter. Maybe you are only doing a particular job or studying something because that is what your parents wanted, or expected, you to do. **Stop living someone else's life. What do you want?** Make sure you are doing what you love, or working towards it, or spending your time outside of work, doing what you love. Maybe you are doing a role because it is easy, or it's all you've ever known. Don't regret never trying something else. Our time on this planet is too precious just to work your 9-5pm for your pay-check, and not be happy. Some people work to live, others live to work, but really, we all should be living with EVERY breath. **Sometimes the menial job is all you need.** You might have enough excitement and things happening outside of work, that keep life interesting for you. I have had many jobs that I haven't enjoyed, however, it has allowed me to seek enjoyment through writing and getting books published, and being able to buy a house etc. Do what you need to, to get you where you need to be. It will be different for each of us. Some of us might be happy being the garbage man, others might aim for other pursuits. **Whatever it is you do with your time, make sure it makes you happy.**

"What lies behind us and what lies before us are tiny matters, compared to what lies within us" Ralph Waldo Emerson

Get sleep, or rest, when you can. Shut your eyes, find silence, then ... find stillness. Meditate, focus on your breathing, get out in nature as much as you can. Once you start feeling connected, you will realise that most of your troubles, are variables that you have no control over, and when you relax and find your focus again you can tackle any outstanding tasks in an orderly fashion. Rest, relax, then focus on each individual task, and show discipline in this process.

Your Greatest Obstacle

"There is nothing so wretched or foolish as to anticipate misfortunes. What madness is it in expecting evil before it arrives" Lucius Annaeus Seneca

Stop over-thinking things, or being too scared to try something; **your worst enemy is all in your head.** If you are to have half a chance to move forward, you must not be defeated before you even begin. Often, we over-think what 'might' happen, assuming the worst, and for fear of ridicule, our ego stops us from even trying in the first place. This happens to all of us at some stage, however, those that succeed, soon learn that only through failure, does success come. It is like buying a lottery ticket, if you don't put yourself in with a chance, you have no chance. Focus on what you want to do. When your mind tries to provide reasons for not following through, cast them aside. Don't let ego or risk of failure stop you from pursuing what you know you want to do. Self-doubt needs to be overcome, so that you can take the steps towards your happiness and **no-one can do it but you!** It doesn't matter how many books you read, or courses you undertake or psychologists that you see, as Morpheus says in the Matrix *"I can only show you the door, you're the one who has to walk through it."*

"The biggest obstacle you will ever have to overcome is your mind. If you can overcome that, you can overcome anything" Les Brown

"Most great people have attained their greatest success just one step beyond their greatest failure" Napoleon Hill

...On Budgeting

"A budget is telling your money where to go rather than wondering where it went" Dave Ramsay

"The best way to stick to a budget, is to start one" Anonymous

Step one: Cut up your cards - get rid of personal loans

This will need to be one of your first priorities. If you have any personal loans, start paying these off, starting with the ones that have the highest interest rate. This spending has to stop, no more personal loans, or if you're thinking about getting one, don't do it! If you have a credit card pay it off. No more purchases.; **cut the cord – cut the card!** These debts will stop you from any savings, and getting yourself to a better position in life. Debt is like a deadweight, dragging you under. No more online shopping, and buying things you don't need. No more shoes, no more Adidas tracksuits, jewellery, no more kids' toys, or cute little shoes. Stop browsing different sites, shopping for things that are of little benefit. If this relates to you, this will be one of the first steps you need to curb in recovery for a new financial future. Repeat after me, no personal loans, no credit cards, just use whatever credit you have in the bank, or in your wallet. This is how to be responsible with your finance, not by playing Russian roulette with lines of credit. By using cards in general, whether it's debit or credit, PayWave and other 'user-friendly' methods, this is moving us away from cash transactions which makes it a lot easier to spend money, and a lot harder to budget. By not physically getting money out of your wallet it seems as if we can make purchases almost guilt-free. There are times when a credit card will be beneficial, such as booking a hotel or a hire car, but it is best to leave it at home on most days (perhaps keep it locked up somewhere) and only use it on those special occasions. Remove the temptation of having it at your fingertips, and **if you do keep a credit card, be sure to put a credit limit on it.** If you are not responsible with one, cut the card and pay any debt off as quickly as possible.

Step 2: Streamline Day-to-day living costs

Write down all your expenses, car service, rego, fuel, rent, shopping, insurances, credit card repayments, child support, cigarettes, Netflix or Spotify account, whatever your situation is. Then write down your weekly income. If your income is less than your expenses, you have a problem and you will need to reduce your expenses – and quickly. How can you save money this week? If you are working or, are out all day, can you take a packed lunch? If you are spending $20 a day for lunch and coffee, 5 days a week for 50 weeks, it is costing you $5,000 each year. Maybe start by getting your weekly shopping done, and then look at what's left; however, this won't work if you can't control your eating habits. Can you not have a beer or smoke on weekdays? Can you maybe not have that punt on the races, or not drop in for that quick $50 on the pokies? Can you avoid online shopping or impulse buys? How do you manage these temptations? How long can you keep chasing the dragon, and following these bad habits. **Know what your weaknesses are - this is where you need to start!** Most people on the breadline, have a vice (well most of us do, no matter where we sit). Whether it's drinking, drugs, sex, gambling, gluttony, or some other sin or indulgence, these are stopping you from achieving your full potential, and you need to break these habits! Can you just have one beer or one cigarette a day, if the answer is no, seek professional help. If you can't get these urges, or bad habits under control, ask for help from relevant support services, A.A, N.A, rehab etc. If your financial situation looks hopeless, seek counselling as soon as possible. If you get to a dark place, phone a friend, or Lifeline. **We all have times where we reach the lowest lows, it's how quickly you can get back up, and dust yourself off, that matters.**

"Debt, an ingenious substitute for the chain and whip of the slave driver" Ambrose Bierce

Miscellaneous Costs (electricity, rates, water)

Don't forget to include these when doing a budget. There is always rent, which, if you live in a share house, you divide, however you also need to discuss electricity and the water bill, and how that will be split. If you are moving to a place on your own, you have to sort out getting power and water put on, and then work out what your average bill is, so that you can budget appropriately. You want to make these the highest priority. Hot water and power are important to healthy living. **If you have just bought your own place, don't forget about rates.** You pay rates to the local council, and you need to factor this in to your budget as well.

If you live in public housing, you will likely have water and power and rent come directly out of your welfare payments, however, don't think this is a similar amount as to what the private rental market is. The rent, and your rates, have been dramatically reduced, so if you want to find your own place, out of your current position in life, you will probably have to consider around double your current cost of living. Perhaps the first step might be finding a job, and moving into a share house. In the meantime, learn how to budget your money, eat healthy foods, and learn all you can from your current position, to then be able to take that next step in the future. It might be serving fish and chips, delivering papers, working at a call centre, cleaning toilets, packing shelves, it doesn't matter what your first (or next) job is, as long as you get some cashflow coming in, and then build from there.

If you can't crunch the numbers, find someone who can! In others words seek help, whether it be a friend or family member, or paid supports. **Be open and honest in your communication.** Tell your trusted friend or relevant person, what you earn, and how you spend your money. How do they manage their money? Do they have tips, like asking the local fruit and vegetable shop if they can have scraps for their pigs or their chickens? Do they go to the supermarket at certain times when there are specials on, maybe Fridays at around 7pm? Do they go out for dinner on cheap Tuesday as their one night out? Review your budget. How many changes could you make to save money for rent, or a house deposit, or a trip overseas?

Back to Shopping – stick to budget! E.g. if you only have a small amount of money, stick to staple products, e.g. milk, bread, rice or noodles, carrots, apples etc. While studying at University I spent many a night living off 2-minute noodles and baby corn from a can. If this is the position that you're in, and you truly want to get out, start with no cigarettes, no drugs, and no alcohol. **There's no time for self-pity … It's time for change!** Another tip is that for everything you buy, don't just look at the specials, look at how much per 100 grams. You can save a great deal of money by being prudent and disciplined. Another challenge, in the vegetables section, is trying to work out whether the price per each broccoli or cauliflower is cheaper than the price per kg. If you're on a budget always get carrots (unless you can't eat carrots) and after the carrots, this is the time you need to look at specials and see what you can afford. If you don't have a fridge can you still perhaps eat some raw beans or cauliflower with your sandwiches? Have you got access to cooking facilities? Soups, noodles, baked beans and spaghetti are all appropriate diets when times are tough. As you get stable income, less debt, and more cashflow, you can treat yourself and start eating a wider variety of food. When this happens, maybe instead of a bottle of green ginger wine a week, you can get a normal bottle of wine, and who knows, maybe eventually a carton of beer a week. Please note these principles are the same no matter what income you earn. You can have a healthy diet, perhaps eat out a few times a week, and work towards saving money for a holiday, or your child's education. If you are gluten free or have any other allergies, it is hard. If you don't have a fridge, it Is even harder still. **Everyone has these money issues, don't compare yourself to others; work with what you've got.** Coffee, buying lunch out, these are luxury items. If you are on a serious budget you will drink instant coffee and eat a packed lunch. Health insurance, gym memberships, customised car mods or number plates, whatever is over and above basic needs will have to stop. If you drive a car, use fuel vouchers where possible. Perhaps car sharing might be an option with a friend, or another student or colleague? If you use public transport, can you travel off peak? Perhaps if you don't have internet at home, you can get a weekly travel pass, and use internet or wi-fi at the local library? **Think outside the square**. You need to work harder than the next person to break your drought and change your situation.

"If broke people are making fun of your financial plan, you're on the right track" Dave Ramsey

Make Your Own Hummus

Seriously, whether it be hummus, or cake, fruit-bars or potato chips, whatever you enjoy eating, (preferably that is good for you) you should learn to make. It will be not only better for your hips, but better for your hip pocket. Sometimes fresh vegetables might be too expensive, so frozen peas might have to do for a while, but if you can make some meals and freeze them, and make soups and slices, depending on what suits your taste buds, do it. It will also keep you active and focused on a particular task. **The worse thing you can do when you are unemployed or feeling low is procrastinate, watch TV, or do nothing at all.** If you have the space, start a garden, even if it's just herbs. Perhaps you can do cherry tomatoes or something small to start with. You will get the satisfaction of growing your own food, as well as saving money at the same time. **The more space you have, the more fruit and vegetables you should try and grow.** If you have the space for chickens and you like eggs, this is another good option.

Don't Overstay Your Welcome

If someone is letting you stay with them for a few days, weeks, months, or even six months; use this time wisely. Save what you can, don't fall in the trap of self-regret by lamenting that you were never given an opportunity. Make one! Work hard, get off the couch, switch off the TV, eat something healthy, exercise, stop hating yourself, do research, ask questions without fear of ridicule. Repeat each day for a month, see what happens and you will get yourself back on track. Life is too short. Spend your time and money wisely.

If this turns into a longer-term arrangement, either get yourself on the lease, or do up a **written agreement** confirming that you will pay a certain amount of rent and water for the period up to the end of the current lease (or whatever arrangement suits). Although your friend/s or housemate/s might just laugh it off, or tell you not to worry, you will then have it all down in writing. It is also important as these sorts of agreements will be what you are dealing with in your future employment, and other types of

written contracts during your life.

Finding and Keeping a Job

Although this figure is constantly increasing, according to the

2017 bureau of labour statistics in America, the average person

changes jobs an average of around twelve times during their

career (https://www.thebalancecareers.com/how-often-do-

people-change-careers-3969407). Because job changes are so

common, it is important for workers to be experts at job

searching and networking. The successful worker is one who is

up-to-date on trends in their industry, while also being well

versed at interviews and being able to connect well with potential

employers.

"He or she who gets hired is not necessarily the one who can do that job best but, the one who knows the most about how to get hired" Richard Lathrop

If it's a job you want, do you know where to look? Don't ever just try one place. The best search engines online are different in each state. In Victoria MyCareer often has more options than Seek, whereas in most states Seek is more commonly used. However, don't discount some of the smaller sites like Indeed, Jobseeker, Jora, and even Gumtree. If you are looking for a government job, they have their own listings in each state, such as: iworkfornsw.gov.au, smartjobs.qld.gov.au, or careers.vic.gov.au. Local papers still list positions, especially for smaller employers. You can drop in to employers like nurseries etc, though most industries will list positions online only. It is also good to personally get some exposure online, putting yourself out there and seeing what might be available. One good option for this is LinkedIn. You can connect with many different people and put forward your areas of interest, and you never know who might get in touch with you with an opportunity. **If you are in rural and remote communities, nothing beats word of mouth.** Let people know you are keen for farm-work, or the meatworks, whatever it might be. Just be ready when opportunity comes your way. We have Seek, MyCareer, Adzuna and CareerOne, as some of the larger sites in Australia, that allow you to upload your details and allow employers to view your details. These sites also provide career advice and structured industry job searches. In America, they use even more comprehensive search engines, such as CareerBuilder and Monster. I am sure it won't be long before this type of system will become more commonplace, so it is important to have a strong CV and eventually build an online profile.

"The difference between ordinary and extraordinary is that little extra" — Jimmy Johnson

Okay so some people might not have internet. That's no excuse. You can use Internet at local libraries, quite often at TAFE, Universities, and definitely with your local employment services agency or Centrelink. If you are going to one of these places **find out when the least busy time is**. If you're not sure, try going there first thing in the morning, or the last hour before closing, so that you can find the time when there are minimal distractions, and there is more chance of getting a computer for a longer period of time. Perhaps mid-morning is the time that there are less people. Try different times, and when there, use your time wisely. Go in with a plan. Maybe first time you go, try and write a cover letter, next time work on your CV, and finally, spend time applying for jobs. What about a friend's place, your parents, who you don't see very often, might have internet that you can use, or have you got a capped plan so that you can use data on your phone without it costing too much? If you are rural or remote, or not working in the city where public transport is readily available – get your licence! This will be vitally important, and rather than wait till you get offered a role that you can't get to, make it a priority **to get your licence as soon as possible.**

Be willing to offer an unpaid work trial to prove yourself in a role. This might be a day, a week, or up to a month, but after this time you should be able to request paid work and if they are not forthcoming, you should move on.

Have you got anchors, keeping you where you are, i.e. kids in school, ageing parents who need your care? If not, do you possibly need to relocate and go somewhere else for work? Perhaps you know someone, or have family, interstate or overseas? Could you go for a holiday, and see what's available there? Maybe working for our defence forces might be a good option to get employment, while also benefiting from training in an area of interest? If you've explored all options where you live, you need to look elsewhere. If you are on welfare, but want to break the cycle - do something different! You might have to travel inland for what might not even be your ideal job, but it is something, and if you have kids, you are setting a good example for what it takes to find work. There are hundreds of employers who would be willing to give you a start, whether it be working on a farm, in a factory, filling shelves at supermarkets, or picking fruit in the middle of summer. You can find out so much information on the internet before you even have to physically go there! You can apply for a role first and if there is an interview, you can arrange a trip. Even if you do have anchors, maybe the perfect job is interstate and it is worth moving the family for? **Be bold, be brave.** You never know what you might find... maybe even yourself!

"Ability is what you're capable of doing, motivation determines what you do, attitude determines how well you do it" Lou Holtz

Early bird gets the worm

Set up job alerts, house alerts, whatever you are looking for. If you are looking for work, get the morning paper early, and check the positions vacant. If there are numbers to call, be one of the first to call. Your willingness for what's on offer, is half the battle. Your willingness to learn, and do the hard yards is your next challenge. Don't complain about possibly doing unpaid overtime, you've at least got a start. If they are riding you, start looking around but, don't jump without a parachute, make sure you have something to go to first. You've come this far, speak to colleagues to see if everyone is having to do unpaid work all the time. Be sure to hang in there, at least until something better comes along. Whether it's a customer, or a colleague, someone will be noticing your work ethic. Nothing you do in this life, is for nothing.

There are more jobs out there than you think

In the city, most businesses advertise, however if you are interested in small businesses (or even franchises), it is worth just turning up, in formal attire, with a resume. In rural and remote towns, most small businesses don't advertise at all; they don't need to. People turn up and they give them a go, and if it works out, they stay on. If you're not the sort of person to just turn up, or you don't have transport, you could go to the local employment service and hopefully get some help. You might get a list of local farmers or businesses in an area you are interested in. Depending on where you are, (or the nearest town you would be happy to relocate to) it might be, blueberries, meatworks, farmhand, sugarcane, wheat, cotton etc. They might just know someone who is looking for workers, and possibly be able to give you a number to call. If you go into any small town, and go to the pub and mention that you are looking for work, most publicans will know of what's around, and point you in the right direction. Put yourself out there and see what you find. Hire-Up and other recruitment organisations that offer contract work, are also good agencies to sign up with. They might only be short-term, but often when you fill a role and prove yourself, management is likely to just keep you on, or they will encourage you to apply for ongoing positions that they know are coming up.

Make sure you at least have a mobile phone number, and some credit on your phone. You'd be surprised how many people don't have a working phone (or voicemail), and even more that never have any credit on their phone, to return calls. If you're serious about finding work, make sure you have phone credit with a cheap monthly phone plan as part of your budget. When you have your phone in order, be sure to answer it! If you miss a call, make sure you have a voicemail set up, and call back at the first opportunity about work. Make sure you don't have a tacky voicemail that is rude or offensive. A childish or offensive voicemail may be the difference between getting a start, or not being given a chance at all.

What industry do you want to be in? Newspapers, radio, supermarket, law, support work, accounting? Go to your nearest work environment of interest, dressed as if you are going for an interview (or just job appropriate attire), and ask if they are looking for staff. Offer to do an unpaid work trial, if they are not initially forthcoming. Ask questions about how to get into the industry, do you need a qualification? Perhaps, if you do a trial, you will impress them so much that they will give you a paid job and cover the cost of the relevant course.

"One's destination is never a place, but rather a new way of looking at things" Henry Miller

Don't Jump Without a Parachute

Changing jobs is fine. People have given me grief or said 'here he goes again' for all my job hopping, but I moved because I was not satisfied and I have high expectations of where I spend most of my waking hours. Your time is precious, so you can't waste it being unfulfilled. You need to be aware of this. However, for all the changing of jobs, I've always made sure I've had a new role to move to before putting in my resignation. Also, in this regard, **the amount of times you can reasonably move is relative to the size of the town or city that you live in**. For example, if you live in a big city, you can make many more moves, than if you are in a small town. I have gained a great deal of experience along the way, much more than if I'd stayed put in positions for five and ten years at a time.

"Until you value yourself, you won't value your time. Until you value your time, you will not do anything with it" M. Scott Peck

Be flexible and try different roles; nothing's permanent in this life. A permanent role can become redundant in a heartbeat. Life's too short to worry about only having a temporary position. This is only going to increase with more contract/temporary employment, but you must always be ready for the next opportunity. I've had many jobs, but I've always found the next rock before my next jump across the stream. Gaps in employment, especially long gaps, will drag you down, help you lose self-esteem and motivation, and make it harder to climb to the next rock. Be willing to take any role or study, to help you reach that next stage of where you want to be.

"Stay positive and happy. Work hard and don't give up hope. Be open to criticism and keep learning. Surround yourself with happy, warm and genuine people" Tena Desae

Here is an example of a Daily plan if you are looking for a job (and a new place to live).

Please note if you are a single parent you need to make sure that you have internet and an online subscription to your local paper and you can follow the steps below from, 'you can now have

breakfast' *(I'm not promoting leaving your kids home alone while you go out).*

This DAY PLAN would be an example of what to do on the weekday that the classifieds for job listings are released. For my local paper the main day for job listings is a Thursday (and there are also jobs listings on a Saturday).

- Get up at 6am (have an alarm set for this time).

- No seriously, stop pressing snooze – GET UP!

- Get dressed into whatever's comfortable and take a walk (preferably for about half an hour).

- On the walk (if possible) buy a newspaper

- If no shops on your walk, either extend your walk to the shop (if it's not too far away). If it's too far, you will need to get a bike (and ride to shops to get a newspaper).

- If it's too far to the shops (i.e. more than 10kms or 20kms bike ride) do you have a car? After your walk (if you have a car) you should drive to the shops. If you can't get the newspaper because you have no car, get an online subscription to your local paper.

- Try to call as soon as possible, to enquire about a position in the paper. **The early bird often gets the worm, particularly for unskilled roles**. If you find a job that you really like, (hopefully you have your phone on you), call the number as soon as you pick up the paper, even if it's 6:30am in the morning. Call ASAP (hopefully after you've paid the shopkeeper) and before you begin your walk/ride back home.

- You might end up leaving a few voicemails for various roles. Make sure you leave your name and number and let them know that you are enquiring about the job and you would appreciate a call back at earliest convenience. This will show you are keen, and puts you in with a chance.

- If you can't get the paper (as above) you will be looking through online classifieds from your local paper, and calling up about any of the jobs that really stand out for you (if you have kids, hopefully before they get up or start nagging you).

- If you went out and are now back home – **you can now have breakfast**

- While having breakfast you can be going through the newspaper and circle ALL the jobs that you can apply for.

If you've been looking online, you will have made notes of the jobs you can apply for, and hopefully you have also begun calling about these positions.

- If you have kids, you will be preparing them for school and making sure they have their lunches (if this all gets too busy, try to prepare their lunchboxes the night before).

- If you have kids, you will obviously deal with last minute tantrums and make sure they get to bus stop etc.

- **NOW, once they have gone,** we take a deep breath and get back to what jobs you circled (or if you are online you will re-open the page on the computer).

- If you've had to do this job search (through your local paper online) and haven't yet been out of the house, now that the kids are gone, and you've (hopefully) already made some calls. Go for a walk. Exercise will help clear your mind and get your energy flow happening.

- Okay if you're still in the 'I need a job more than anything else' phase, you can go online (at home or go into the community, library, employment services etc.) Hopefully you have a USB, or a CV (and maybe cover letter) saved on your email. Work your way through job search sites, Seek, MyCareer, Monster, Jora, Indeed, Gumtree, and apply for ANYTHING that you are capable of doing.

- Hang on you might be thinking, why apply for so many jobs, when I might get a call back from the first newspaper job? You can never be certain, particularly if you are desperate for employment and have been out of work for some time. It is otherwise known as the scattergun approach, and this is what it takes, if you don't want to wait too long!

- **Lunch** – you need to eat, to keep the mind active. It must be close to lunchtime now. Relax, take a breath. Listen to some music and congratulate yourself. It's been a productive morning.

- If finding a job and finding a new place to live are both required, you can do the above step, or this step, in either order, depending on priority. You will be heading into town now (especially if you had a computer at home and did the above step in the comfort of your own home). You will first go to real estate places and get their weekly listings for property. You might even go to the local community centre, TAFE, or University, or even shopping centres have noticeboards that sometimes have flyers for people looking for other tenants (depending on if you want to live with others).

- As a next step (depending on your situation) you might want to apply for Community Housing. The time should be well after lunch-time now (which is good because they are short-staffed over lunch, and you might not get the support you might need). You will be given a whole bunch of paperwork to apply for public housing. Rather than getting too overwhelmed, find out what is needed to go along with these forms (e.g. copies of licence, or passport, electricity bills, in your name, bank statement, or any other identification) and also ask if there is a best time/day (as soon as possible), that you can come back and get some assistance with completing the forms.

- Oh, look at the time, you have to be home to meet the kids at the bus stop, or, even if you don't have kids, you should be exhausted by now. It's time to head home.

- You've just done maybe a 6-3pm day, in most cases, more than a day's work! Does it feel good, well, it might just feel tiring, but you've done your best to improve your situation. Pat yourself on the back. But we're not done just yet.

- You may make a call (or two) before 7pm, to enquire about some places for rent (if there were any of interest on the community board or elsewhere).

- For bed-time reading (or whenever you can have a moment to yourself) you will review the rental listings, circling (or I like to use a highlighter), any places that may be suitable. Going to see the real estate companies will form part of tomorrow's plan (unless it's the weekend), along with getting documents for community housing ready (if you are going to explore that option). If so, you will need to complete as much of it as you can, and then go in to their office (at the time they advised was the best time), to get some assistance completing the forms. They will make every effort to help you complete the forms, particularly if you turn up at their suggested day and time.

Please note that you need to be willing to consider ALL locations to give you the best chance of finding something. In Northern NSW and the Tweed Heads region, the waiting list can be around ten years or longer, so consider any options more inland, or less sought after, if you don't want to wait such a long time.

On day 2 – you might also need some help from Employment Services or a recruitment company. Go in and get connected. There is a hidden job market out there and you may find opportunities that are not listed online or in the paper, and besides, why should you have to do all the leg-work!

Are There Other Ways for You to Earn a Quid?

No, I'm not talking about the black market or the sex industry. Have you got family who run a business, who can give you some weekend, or night work? Has someone close to you got land they are not using, that you could use, because maybe you are passionate and know a lot about vegetables? Are you a whiz on editing, and can get contract work online, perhaps surveys, reviews, or graphic design work?

Some work that is paid in meals and accommodation will still allow you to access welfare. This is a good opportunity to get in the right headspace, gain confidence and new skills, and make sure you are job-ready for the next opportunity that comes along. You might end up staying on in this sort of role because you like it so much. At the current time of writing, you can earn up to $104 a fortnight, and still get your Centrelink payments. Part of the work contract might include accommodation and meals, so it actually might be a pretty reasonable deal! For those brave enough to head west, and take on some different work, you will gain excellent skills and perhaps acquire that aptitude that will help you in any venture you take in the future, although you might even find this sort of arrangement in regional town and smaller cities.

CV's and Cover Letters:

Job service providers can help with your CV, or, (if you are capable on the internet) find yourself a basic template online and go from there. If you have a friend who is good with this sort of thing, perhaps you could give them some guitar lessons, or help them in some way, if they can help you. Here are some other tips in regards to your CV:

- Try to keep your CV between 1 - 3 pages.
- Don't put too many colours or images in it (no more than 2 colours or 1 image)

I understand wanting to set your CV apart in some way, but don't fall into that trap. Keep it simple. Resumes and references are much less important than the interview itself, but you still need to make it to the interview. Make sure you include all work (or volunteer work), with your most recent first. As a general rule, don't include more than your last ten years. Keywords, are also becoming more important in regards to writing your CV. These are the words (in particular industries) that the Employer wants to know, that you know about. Keywords are more relevant for skilled roles that require qualifications, so if that's what you are applying for, you will need to consider keywords in your CV. There is a great deal of literature about identifying and using keywords in Resumes. For further details on the importance of keywords, take a look at: https://www.squawkfox.com/8-keywords-that-set-your-resume-on-fire/

References

The general consensus is that you leave your referees off your

Resume. If you list your references on the resume, you run the

risk that one (or more) of the people screening the resume might

know one of your contacts and might not like, or respect your

reference. They may wrongly assume that you listed a friend, as

opposed to the persons listed being genuine non-biased

supervisors. Unfortunately, people stereotype and pass

judgement, so you want to remove any of this possible risk. There

is also the chance that the employer will call the references

before speaking to you, and that they will not be impressed with

what is said. If your resume makes it past the first scan, you want

the employer to be calling you, not another person, which might

take you out of consideration, without them even speaking to

you. Therefore, leave references off your resume. You may simply

say 'to be advised' or 'available upon request'. By doing this you

will get to sell yourself in an interview and then be able to provide

the references to support you afterwards. Of course, they may

still make these assumptions about your referee, or not receive

good feedback, but hopefully you have advised your referee by this stage, and you have enough awareness to know if they will provide a good reference, and besides, hopefully you woo-ed the employer enough in the interview anyway.

The important factors for your referees are:

- Most recent and most senior (that are going to speak highly of you)
- Sometimes you can use your current manager (if you have one). Be careful with this though, as it will depend on whether you are only a casual, or a permanent staff member, and also whether you have a good rapport with your Manager. If you are unsure, err on the side of caution and don't put them down.
- If you don't have any Managers or supervisors that you can use, colleagues will have to do.
- If you are applying for your first job out of school, your year advisor or school principal might be an option, or alternatively a character reference from a sporting coach,

or last resort, friend of the family. Character references are generally not advised (unless you can get one from Richard Branson).

- Written references in this day and age are also not commonly used, however if that is all you have (because your previous Manager has moved on or cannot be located) then go with it.

The Cover Letter

I don't generally like them, but they do give you a chance to sell yourself and are an important part of the application process. Start by doing a Google search on 'cover letters' to get general templates to help you draft a standard cover letter. This will obviously need to be adapted for each role that you apply for. Make sure the cover letter is no more than a page. Use keywords that they may have used in their job description, and for most positions, you will want to identify with how the values of the organisation fit with you, and why this position appeals to you.

You also want to show what transferable skills or knowledge that you can bring to the role. Have you used the same systems, worked in a similar team structure, dealt with the same council or government policies and procedures? Do you have the appropriate tickets or licences? Also make sure you spell-check your CV and cover letter before sending it through to the employer. Perhaps a recruitment agency or employment service representative can proof read your cover letter and CV before you start sending it out?

In Regards to Interviews

Most people either hate interviews, or, have done enough of them that they are not completely filled with trepidation. They are nerve-racking, there is no doubt about it, you just have to be as prepared as you can be, and c'est la vie. **99% of interviews will have very similar formats.** There will either be a question about *'what do you know about the company?'* or, *'why are you the best person for the job?'* They will likely ask you to, *'tell us of a situation where you had to'* ... (depending on the role, it could be... *'manage competing priorities, 'deal with difficult customers', 'manage a major project', 'dealt with an emergency situation', 'work with complex systems')*. There is almost always a question, *'describe how you have been flexible in one of your previous roles'*. Basically, this is saying the role isn't going to be what was in the job description, you'd better be able to handle change, or, you are not going to cut it. Make sure you have prepared answers beforehand for the above types of questions. They may not be exactly the same questions, but you will be able to get the majority of your answers in the interview, from the above. If you have answered key selection criteria for the role, read over what your responses were. These questions will also give you some indication of what the focus areas of the interview will entail.

Many organisations expect responses to be in the STAR format which is:

Situation – Give an example of a time when you had to … (i.e. deal with difficult customer)

Task – What were your tasks/duties? Did you go above what was expected of you?

Action - what actions did you take to resolve the situation (i.e. calmed customer down, used active listening, repeated their concerns, followed up to make sure they were satisfied etc).

Response – i.e. positive feedback from your Manager, your assistance helped reduce the number of customer complaints, or, the result of a change in procedures due to you identifying issues in general processes.

Over time you will have built up a repertoire that can be used for any situation. You will feel more and more confident because you know that you can answer any question that is thrown at you because you have prepared responses, written them down, read and re-read them until they just pop out in the interview. When this happens the ums and ahs and nervous twitches stop, and you will give yourself every opportunity of getting the job, once you have made it to the interview stage.

What to Say

Depending on what job you are going for, you might have one person, or a few people interviewing you. Sometimes you need to keep it to the point, *'where have you worked before, why do you want to work here; how do you deal with change or conflict?'* Other times they will ask you about yourself, or ask you to *'describe a situation when'*. Prior to the interview be sure to closely review all the details that are listed on the job description. Make sure you look up the company, check their website, and make dot points on a small piece of paper that you can read over just before you go in for the interview. This will ensure that it will all be at the front of mind, and you'll say everything that you need to. You will also need to make sure that you have some key points that you want to get across at some stage during the interview. You don't want to go into life details, where you grew up, that you come from a traditional family etc. however, you will need to let them know briefly, what your work history is, your positive traits (i.e. "I get along well with people from all backgrounds" and "I am a good communicator") as well as all of your transferable skills.

If it's an **administration job**, you'll need to have some strong computer skills, and preferably have completed a course. Advise them of this, and anything exceptional you did, or possibly, feedback that you received. You don't want to sound like a smart arse, but this will show that you have attention to detail, and that you take your work and study seriously. If it's a **retail role** you need to advise how you've dealt with customers, and have an example of dealing with a difficult customer. Some **blue-collar roles** it will be just having the required ticket, a current licence, car and the availability to start tomorrow! What you say will depend on what role you're being interviewed for, however make sure you let them know everything that would be relevant for the position. You don't want to walk out and think to yourself; 'I should have told them about that online course I did in marketing'. Even if it's a retail role, perhaps they have another role coming up, or they are looking for someone who also has that particular type of experience that you mentioned.

Some tips for the interview itself:

- If you get nervous, practice interview questions beforehand, with any family or friends.
- Don't be late for an interview; allow for train or bus delays
- Handshake (not too firm)
- Smile and make eye contact with each person in the room
- If there are a panel of people interviewing you, and they each alternate with their questions, make sure you (at

least) look at the person asking the question with each response.

- Hide your nervousness. This is often a giveaway with your hands, so hold them together or under the desk (out of sight).

- Don't get side-tracked and talk too much

- Limit ums, and ahs

- Know something about the company. Quite often they will ask why you want to work there, it might be their reputation, they might be family-owned, or have a focus on conservation. Know their values and when the company originated, at the bare minimum.

- Stick to the question, repeat the question if you have to, or, if the interviewer starts looking at you strangely, get confirmation that you are on the right track.

- Stick to a planned response i.e. STAR, for situational questions, *"can you tell me a time when..."* (Situation), describe where you were, the (Task) involved, (Action) taken, and (Response) i.e. the feedback for what you did.

If it is easier you can just use, **who** was involved, **what** was done, **where** and **when** did it happen, **why** was it done (what was the end result?).

- Don't use jargon, acronyms or lingo that may not be understood in the interview.
- Stay calm, if it's not meant to be, something else will come along.
- Negotiating salary and hourly rate should only occur AFTER a job is offered to you.

What to wear

Have a nice formal set of clothes for your interview. You want to wear one step above what you would wear for the job itself. For office jobs, a suit and tie (weather permitting) is a good option (at least a plain long-sleeved short with a tie, if it's summer-time). If it's retail, or even hospitality, it still wouldn't hurt to overdress.

In summary:

- Overdress (in formal clothes) if you're a male – wear a tie.
- If you're a woman, keep it formal, or wear attire that is appropriate to the role, and

- In general, make sure that you are neat and tidy.

For blue collar roles, don't be too concerned. I don't know too many plumbers, labourers or concreters who turned up for interviews dressed differently from what they would wear on a worksite. For other roles, if you are dressed appropriately, you are half-way there. It will help with your confidence, and reduce anxiety, also. I have one shirt that I wear to every interview. It has close to fifty interviews under its belt (or my belt), and for each interview, I am as prepared (and comfortable) as I can be.

First Impressions Count

Make a good first impression. Sometimes you need to cut your hair, tuck in your shirts, have a shave, and make sure that you have put deodorant on. Polish your shoes, and if you are a male, and you are applying for non blue-collar roles, did I mention - wear a tie. People stereotype. Don't change who you are, but there are certain expectations for an interview. Spend time on your CV initially and then, when offered an interview, you need to have a suitable work-ready appearance, when meeting potential employers. If you are going to do a CV drop off, be sure to dress as if you are going to get to speak to the Manager on the spot. Be prepared to talk about yourself and try and have one thing you know about that particular employer. Maybe they've changed their name, or maybe they just changed their façade and branding, once again, just be ready for whatever situation arises. You might need to take a deep breath and steady yourself before going in and asking to speak to the Manager, but if you do get to speak to them, you just need to be ready.

"In the middle of difficulty, lies opportunity" Albert Einstein

After the Interview:

Last impressions Count. If you miss out on a role and they have just called to let you know, **thank them for their time** and take on board any feedback that they have given you. You never know, if the other person doesn't take the job, they might be so impressed with your attitude and positive communication that they may call you back again, but with some better news this time. It also puts you in good stead for future roles that could come up within their organisation. **If unsuccessful in an interview remember to ASK for feedback if it is not forthcoming**. I am not the biggest fan of asking for feedback, but it is important. Sometimes, you will actually get something of value, such as, *"unfortunately you lacked the qualifications needed in this particular area"*, or *"we required more practical knowledge of this particular system"*. These bits of feedback are gold, because they tell you what areas you need improvement in. Other times you will just get feedback that is generic and beige, that offers nothing specific and would just be a standard response to all interviewees, such as, *"unfortunately there was someone with more experience"*. Remember to ask for feedback, because if you do get something specific, as to why you were not successful, you know what to work on for next time.

When You Have a Job

How do your values align with the company that you are working for?

If you find a good boss, or make good friends with work colleagues, maybe your job isn't so bad. I've had some excellent bosses and some absolutely horrible ones. The ones I have had the upmost respect for have treated me with respect, and as an equal, and I have stayed in positions that I have hated, for a lot longer than I should have, because of a good boss, or having good people around me. What is your work culture like? Do you genuinely get along with at least one work colleague? If so, this is a good start. Your boss can be good at what they do, but are they a good manager? Do they care about you, ask how you are going, or, when things are bad, do they enquire about home life with genuine concern? Sure, there are some jobs you just need to turn up and get the job done and that's okay, but if it's a job with a lot of interaction, and there is no care factor from your Manager, is this the place for you?

Efficient and Effective

I've heard all the clichés for work, KPI's, SWOT, SME, BAU, WIP, COB, EOD, EOM, OTP, WOM, POC, PEST, OGSM, LPO, KISS, or the six P formula, just to name a few. I've often been told to be more efficient and effective, work smarter not harder, failing to plan is planning to fail, I've undertaken 360-degree reviews, train the trainer, developed contingencies, and considered external variables in performance management. I've also heard almost every other acronym under the sun, though at the end of the day, everything you are told to do, is helping management review and critique all aspects of your work. Phone call monitoring, assessing keywords, time on phone, getting person's contact details, creating marketing lists for future calls or SMS's, cold-calling, chasing prospective leads, all forms of marketing strategies, including assessment of the online footprint of customers. You need to be aware that we are just a cog in the wheel, and with this awareness, the next step is to find out where you want to fit, in this puzzle of life. Are there new markets emerging that you could be a part of, that are more socially conscious? How will you find a job where you are comfortable, and eventually, where you can be your own boss? Is that what you want, or are happy with just doing your current job, and enjoying your freedom at knock-off time? There are so many questions, and **the only right answer, is what is right for you.**

The Age of Entitlement

Stop expecting everything to be given to you. We live in the age of entitlement; sad but true. You will meet a lot of people who say; 'this should be free, that should be included, what else can you give me?' They will complain, to try and get free stuff, and blame everyone but themselves, for their predicament. You need to do something different, unless you want to deal with Centrelink for the rest of your life, and if you do continue on this path, you are most likely leading your children on that same path. **Prove yourself and go out and earn it, don't expect it all to be given to you**. This will give you a whole new lease on life and, when you are contributing, it will help you get a taste of real fulfillment. If you've ever given your time, or money to something and expected nothing in return, you will have gotten a true taste of the joy of giving. In giving ourselves, we learn one of the most valuable lessons in life. **The 'poor me' attitude, will get you nowhere**. No more regrets, and living in the past, today is the day you live for the future. Whatever has happened, whatever you have just missed out on has gone, let it go, don't cling to it. **The only time that matters is right now.**

*"**If you are depressed, you are living in the Past. If you are anxious, living in the future. If you are at peace you are living in the moment**"* Lao Tzu

General Advice

Healthy Living

Find hobbies that benefit you and that are healthy for your body, or your soul (or both). Go for a walk, ride a bike, learn to surf, read a book, draw, listen to music, join a soccer team, whatever you can do that you will enjoy and won't take you off your course to where you can achieve your full potential. Make sure that if you are going into an employment service, or dropping in to see employers, that you have deodorant on and you have cleaned your teeth. General hygiene is important to selling yourself, so that you can have the best chance possible at getting a start. It may sound obvious, but you'd be surprised how many people have turned up dishevelled and unkempt for interviews, where the job was theirs, but after the meeting, the Manager has had second thoughts. Look after yourself, be prepared and be ready, because once you've got yourself a job, any job, you can always prepare for the next stepping stone, to get you where you want to be.

Take a Walk in Others Shoes

A different perspective will give you a new lease on life. I remember going to Egypt and seeing how poor some people really are. They were impoverished, flyblown, almost corpses begging for money. Some were missing limbs, and the dust rose from the earth and covered them, like a blanket. It was hard returning to our lucky country and realising what they would give to be provided with just a roof over their head and one square meal a day. In Australia, this is available to anyone and everyone who goes looking (though it might not be in the location that everyone wants to be in). **Being on welfare should be a means to an end, not the final destination.** This sunburnt country, and land of sweeping plains, has plenty of employers who will take on those willing. **How far have you gone out of your comfort zone?** The next town to where you grew up in? The nearest city? Another state? another country? If you're stuck, think of everyone you know who lives elsewhere, where could be a suitable destination for you to visit, and see what opportunities are available?

Have You Ever Thought About a Move?

While most of us in Australia continue to hug the coastal fringes and complain that we can't get a job, or can't find affordable housing, here's an idea. GO WEST! Just over the range on the way to Moree there's a place called Gravesend. Apart from the slightly depressing name, a 3-bedroom house is going for $110,000 (you might even get them down to under $100k). Alternatively (in April 2019), you could buy 2,023m² of land at Warialda for $9,900. The land would be cheaper than the old caravan you might want to put on it! **Actually, at the time of writing, after looking at properties online, every state in Australia has an option to buy a house for under $100k.** Broken Hill had a house for sale for $45k, and a place in Monto was selling for $50k! See, anyone can be a home or landowner (if that's one of your goals), you've just got to be willing to consider a change of location. You can create a new life for yourself, if you're willing to show some courage, and take a leap of faith.

Follow the Leader

Follow the person, whether it be someone from a bank, real estate, accountant, lawyer, or any paid professional who you have built genuine rapport with, and who you trust. If they are staying in the same industry, follow them and simply change the provider you do business with, so that you continue to work with them. Good help can be hard to come by, and when you find good people, stick with them, and they will help you along the way.

No Interest Loans Scheme (NILS)

When you have no money and nowhere to go, you can look at such organisations as 'The Good Shepherd Microfinance,' who offer no interest loan schemes. They also offer a range of other options for people who need a hand, setting up their own business. If you get a no interest loan – use it wisely, and make sure you budget effectively to make sure you get yourself back on your feet. Don't waste this helping hand you've been given. Other countries also offer no interest loans, i.e. in America, 'The Bank of America', so speak to your bank first in regards to what they can offer, and they should be able to give some advice and point you in the right direction. Although it might seem like people are putting up stop signs, or they are being difficult, it is often just the confines or boundaries, that the person has to work within. They are not against you; they want to be helpful. Don't get upset, listen closely, take heed of any advice that they give, and keep moving forward.

Starting Wage

If you have just finished a degree, or any training course and you get given details of what you should earn first year out, or second year, or after five years, ignore whatever is written. Don't, I repeat, DO NOT trust guides for starting wages (unless you are going into a structured profession like teaching, nursing, law, engineering, or some such profession). This was another point of frustration when after five years I was only getting what was meant to be my starting salary (with the only benefit being a delay in paying off a HECS debt).

How do Interest Rate Rises Effect You?

It may not have much of an effect on you unless you own a house, however the person you are renting from may well increase the rent to cover the extra cost they are paying on their mortgage. If you do own a house an example of how this will affect you is, if you have a $400,000 loan and you are on a flexible loan, which goes up by 0.25% (or quarter of a percent) to 5%, you are paying an extra $1,000 per year (or $19.23 extra per week). Not so bad right? If you get three rate rises a year, or a bigger interest rate hike, thing's start getting tight (and you might already be at the tightest you can be). There are still other options, including refinancing (if you were paying principal and interest, you can just pay principal for a certain period of time). Just remember, what goes up, must come down. Whereas our parents had 18% interest rates, and $30,000 houses, it has been a different ball game, with most of us only experiencing 8% maximum interest rates, though our house prices in many areas are starting at $350,000, and often twice that in the city!

Death and permanent disability insurance and income protection

Most superannuation companies will allow you to have some form of insurance in the case of major accidents where you are seriously injured, or worse. It is highly recommended that you look into these options once you have gained employment, and if needed, get advice from a financial advisor.

Enduring Power of Attorney / Enduring Guardian

An enduring power of attorney is a legal authorisation to act on someone else's behalf in legal and financial matters which continues after the person granting it loses mental capacity. It can therefore be used to manage the affairs of people who have lost the ability to manage on their own. For peace of mind, it is important to have your financial affairs in order in case a major accident occurs in which you are mentally incapacitated. When you put in place an enduring power of attorney it will continue until death, or until you revoke it (if you are capable). It is good to consider your financial matters, as you get older, particularly if you have children. It is recommended that you speak to your solicitor or get further advice about this, depending on your personal situation.

An **Enduring Guardian** is the person you appoint to make health, lifestyle and medical decisions for you when you are not capable of doing this for yourself. Advance Care Directives set out your directions, wishes and values that need to be considered before medical decisions are made on your behalf. Make sure that you speak to a Solicitor about both an Enduring Power of Attorney and Enduring Guardian, particularly as you get older, so that you know that your affairs, and major health decisions, can be looked after by someone that you trust.

Till Death do us Part

A marriage is a financial partnership, just as much as it is an emotional and legally binding partnership. In most cases an innocent (or financially savvy) partner can be liable for the debts of the other. When you have joint accounts and joint credit cards, one person's spending can be the other's burden. Be sure that you work on a budget together, and curb any excessive spending. If you are both on the same page, you will have successfully navigated one of the major roadblocks that can cause issues in maintaining a happy marriage.

Investing with Friends, or Family?

Investing with friends may seem like a great idea, but things can go sour very quickly when one partner has a change of heart, or change of circumstances, and they need to get out quick. It is better to play it safe and just speak to the bank about getting an investment loan for a business opportunity that you are seeking.

Is it worth losing a close friend, or family member, over a business prospect? If you still want to go ahead with this option, make sure you discuss all possible scenarios, just in case the worse-case scenario, does happen.

If You Have a Home Loan - Fixed or Variable?

If you are in a position where you have a mortgage the best advice that I can give is to keep your home loan at a variable rate. I have locked in a high rate at 8% for a maximum period and saw rates plummet to 4%. If you get approval to get a mortgage then you have gotten through the first hurdle. Don't lock yourself into a fixed rate. There might be an increase in rates, but it's better to shop around and get the best variable rate that you can, rather than lock in at a fixed rate. I am not a financial advisor though, so if you are unsure and want a second opinion, speak to a financial advisor and see what they recommend, as your individual circumstances might require the certainty of a fixed rate.

How Does a Recession Effect You?

Employers, especially small businesses, may struggle with stagnant growth and limited opportunities. Export markets may dry up, and there will likely be a reduction in manufacturing and produce with the reduced cashflow. Hopefully you have a job that is stable during these times. It is certainly not a time for moving around too much. If you are an investor, with shares, stocks, or properties, it may actually wipe out a decent chunk of your earnings, or more likely, reduce your net worth, equity and overall worth. However, material wealth, should be of minimal interest as long as you are able to continue to provide for your family. For most of us, a recession will not make a whole lot of difference in our life, you will just hear a lot about the doom and gloom on the news. Hopefully you are paving the way to your new independent life and, in most cases, it shouldn't be of too great concern a concern for you. If you are trying to get a home loan at this time, you will need to have a solid deposit and a stable job because banks will tighten their lending practices.

Don't Judge, or Stereotype

As I write this, I just lost a friend to suicide. He was the guy who everyone looked up to. Larger than life, life of the party... the least likely. He had so many friends, he was smart, well settled in a relationship, the world at his fingertips. This is the perfect example of never judging a book by its cover. We only ever see about 10% of most people. When you see that person across the street, all dressed up, with the flash car and waving money around, don't pass judgement. They might have a terminal illness, or, be suicidal themselves. Money and fashion and even positions of power, don't portray who you really are. Be grateful that you are alive, and that you have clean air and water. One of my closest friends said a few years ago, that his new year's resolution was to keep breathing. He had been going through a rough patch and the honesty of his words took our breaths away. Don't be envious of others positions, or wish you were in someone else's shoes. You don't know what they've been through, or, are going through. Focus on yourself and finding your happiness. It will take hard work, on your body, mind and your soul, but if you commit to it, and not let other distractions get in your way, you will find out who you truly are. If you are on that slippery slope yourself make sure you seek help from friends, family or professional services such as Lifeline.

"Happiness is not the absence of problems; it is the ability to deal with them" Steve Maraboli

Who Loves You?

If you don't have within your answer, **you**, then that is the place to start. You must respect and learn to love yourself. Maybe you've made some wrong decisions and wish you'd chosen a different path. Now is the time to walk that different path. Believe in yourself. **You can't love someone else, before you love yourself.** Eventually you will love each day, each breath, and love and appreciate everything in your life. Start small. It's like when you say you fall in love, that is a state, however when life is full of love... that is a constant. It changes your viewpoint and permeates your very soul. **Work on yourself first.** For example, perhaps you can be more kind, make an effort to do a good deed a day, ask a friend if they need help (or a stranger). It will do you the world of good, and make you start appreciating yourself and your worth.

"To fall in love with yourself, is the first secret to happiness"

Robert Morley

Stay Positive

This is probably the most important of all the advice in this book. If you can't keep a positive mindset, you will not be able to find what you want. The longer you are out of work, or in a place you don't want to be, the harder it is to keep a positive mind. Hang in there. Each missed job, is a learning opportunity. **Don't be too hard on yourself**. Once you dwell on self-pity and regrets, it is hard to break out of this cycle. If the glass isn't half full, you have a problem. **Find the joy in life, and find time each day to do something you love.** When you are happy it will shine forth and help you on your way. Don't let misfortunes and loss of family, friends or pets keep you down for too long. A grieving period is needed, but we must get ourselves back on track when we can. You have a gift, you just need to find what it is, and then live it!

"Whether you think you can, or think you can't, you are right"
Henry Ford

Don't give up before you've even started! Write a list of what you are going to do today. Check local classifieds, go to a job provider and get help with your resume. Get the rental property lists from real estate agents. Check the noticeboard in shopping centre for jobs, accommodation, used cars, whatever you are looking for. Job search online, i.e. Gumtree, Seek, Jora, MyCareer, and ask your friends if they can check with their work, if they have any vacancies. When you've had days where you have tried these options, it is only a matter of time before opportunity arises. Offer to do an unpaid work trial and give it your all. Do not complain or compare to others working there. **Prove yourself and paid work will be the end result.**

"Go confidently in the direction of your dream. Live the life you have imagined" Henry Thoreau

www.ingramcontent.com/pod-product-compliance
Lightning Source LLC
Chambersburg PA
CBHW030651220526
45463CB00005B/1723

* 9 7 8 1 6 9 1 1 3 0 7 2 6 *